UNTAMED
GROSSOLOGY

ICKY THINGS IN THE GREAT OUTDOORS

BY
SYLVIA BRANZEI

ILLUSTRATED BY
JACK KEELY

GROSSET & DUNLAP

GROSSET & DUNLAP
An imprint of Penguin Random House LLC
1745 Broadway, New York, New York 10019

First published in the United States of America by Grosset & Dunlap,
an imprint of Penguin Random House LLC, 2025

Visit us online at penguinrandomhouse.com.

Library of Congress Cataloging-in-Publication Data is available.

Manufactured in China

ISBN 9780593752470   10 9 8 7 6 5 4 3 2 1 TOPL

Design by Kimberley Sampson

THIS BOOK IS DEDICATED TO BINO, AUTUMN, AND ALL BUDDING GROSSOLOGISTS—SB AND JK

A GROSS INTRODUCTION

It's a gross world! This is a great thing if you are a budding grossologist, or a person who studies everything gross. This book contains little bits of information related to the great outdoors. Hmmm . . . maybe related to the icky, disgusting, yucky parts of the outdoors would be more accurate.

After reading this book, you will never see nature the same way again! But, hey, it is all natural. And it is all Grossology.

So many gross things to find out and so little time. So, you better turn the page and get gross!

TABLE OF CONTENTS

6

SQUIRTY AND SQUISHY
MOSQUITOES

MOSQUITOES ARE ACTUALLY A TYPE OF FLY.

- There are over 3,600 different types of mosquitoes.

- If a female mosquito smells a nearby blood meal, she will most likely attack anyone wearing red, orange, black, or greenish-blue.

- A female mosquito's saliva contains a blood-thinning chemical so she can suck the blood up. That is, if you don't swat her first.

- Females are the only bloodsuckers (female mosquitoes, that is). Male mosquitoes eat plant nectar.

7

BEES

HONEY IS ACTUALLY BEE PUKE. BEES COLLECT PLANT NECTAR, GO HOME, PASS IT FROM BEE MOUTH TO BEE MOUTH, SQUIRT IN A BIT OF CHEMICAL, THEN RRRAAALLLFFF—OUT COMES YUMMY HONEY.

- Honeybee hives can have up to 80,000 bees.

- Bumblebees have stinky feet. They use the smelly footprints to tell if it is their footprint, the footprint of a bee relative, or that of a stranger.

- Bees have a venom sac filled with poison. A stinging honeybee loses its venom sac and stinger when it stings. The bee dies shortly after. Other bees, as well as wasps and hornets, don't lose their stinger and can sting multiple times.

- Apitherapy is an alternative therapy that uses bee products, including bee venom, for many human ailments.

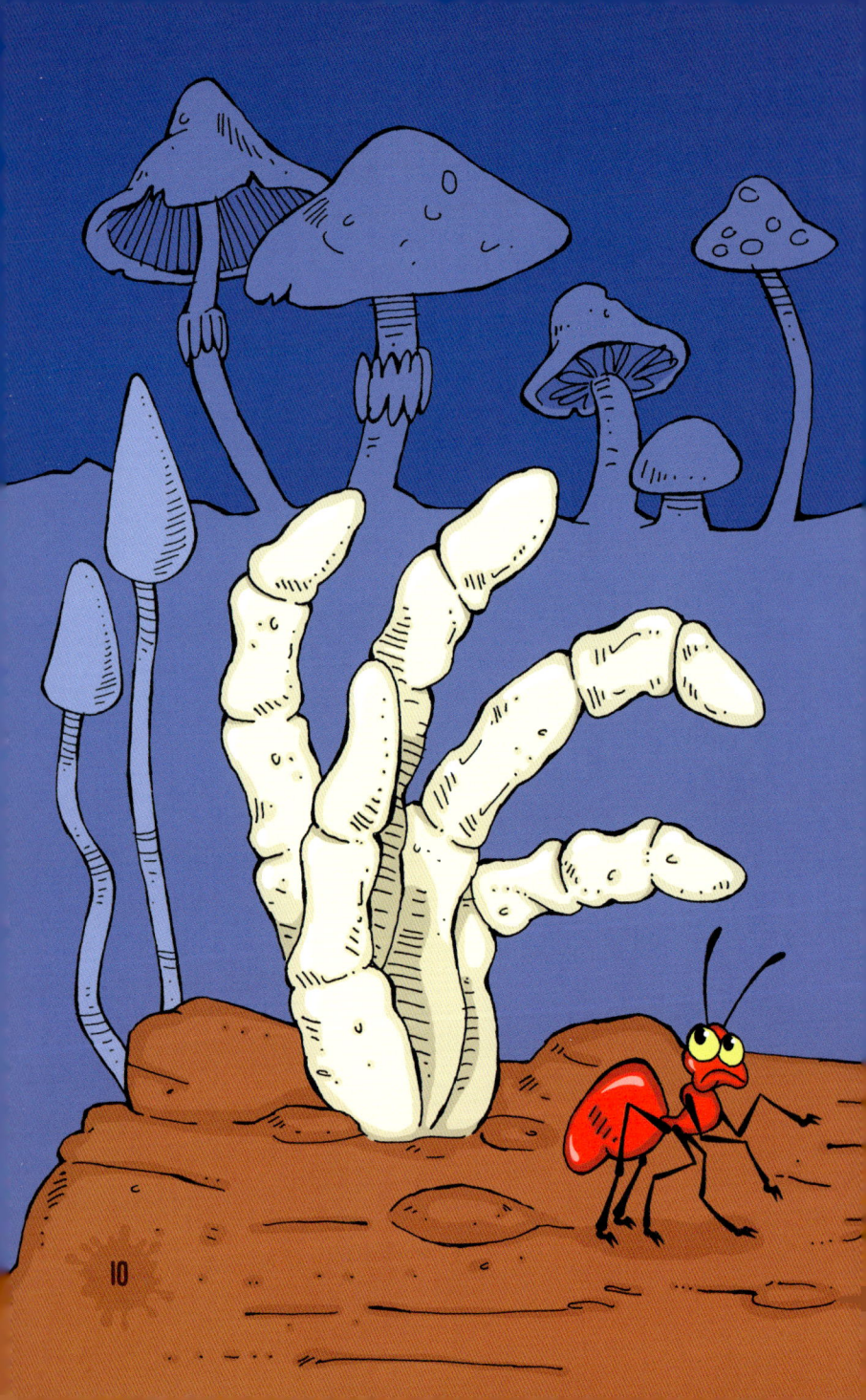

FUNGI

THERE ARE MORE THAN 150,000 DIFFERENT TYPES OF FUNGI KNOWN. MOLD, LIKE THE STUFF THAT GROWS ON SPOILED FOOD, IS A TYPE OF FUNGUS. MUSHROOMS ARE A TYPE OF FUNGUS.

- One type of fungi is called cordyceps, and it can turn insects into zombies. Here's how it works: If a spore—another name for a fungus egg—lands on an insect, it sends out shoots that spread through the insect's organs and change its behavior. The insect has the urge to crawl to a spot about a foot off the ground, where it dies. A stalk erupts through the body and shoots spores down to land on insects below.

- *The Last of Us*, a popular video game and TV show, is based on a fictional mutated cordyceps fungus, or zombie fungus, that infects humans.

- Stinkhorn mushrooms ooze out a goop. The goop smells like putrid animal flesh or poop. Humans find it repulsive, but flies are attracted to it.

- The fungus called dead man's fingers looks like corpse fingers reaching out of a rotting tree.

FLIES

WE KNOW OF MORE THAN 90,000 DIFFERENT TYPES OF FLIES, AND THEY CAN BE FOUND MOST EVERYWHERE ON LAND—INCLUDING ANTARCTICA.

- Maggots are the worm stage of flies that live by eating dead and decaying stuff.

- In some countries, people munch on sun-dried maggots.

- Some types of flies decapitate ants! One type of parasitic fly hunts down an injured ant, uses specialized mouth parts to saw off the head, and then lays her eggs in the ant head.

- There are flies that look like spiders and bees. The female bee-fly sprays out eggs like a machine gun around ground-dwelling bees. The fly eggs hatch, and the maggots sneak into the bee nest and eat the newly hatched bee grubs.

13

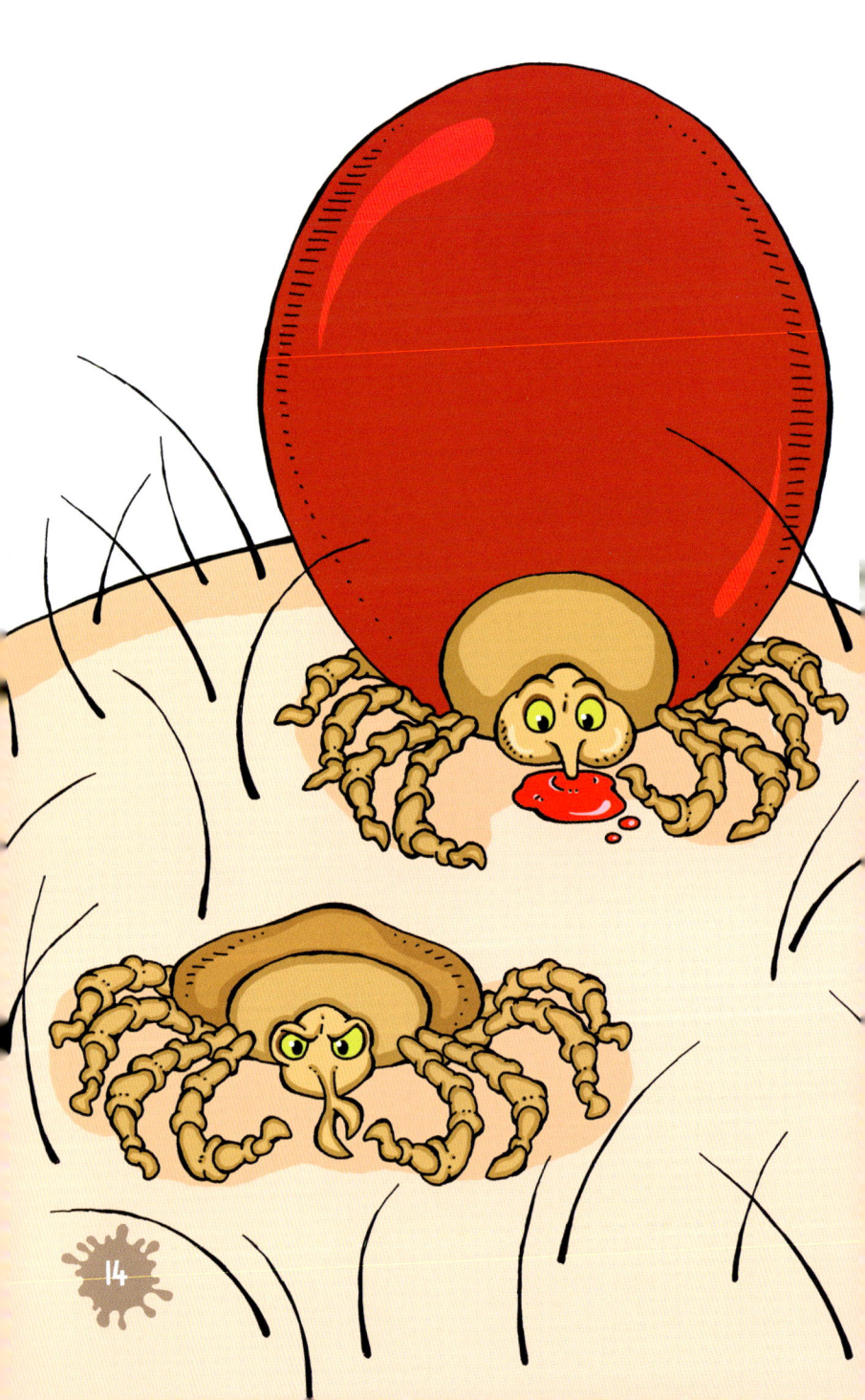

TICKS

TICKS ARE ARACHNIDS THAT LIVE BY ATTACHING TO AND SUCKING THE BLOOD FROM WARM-BLOODED ANIMALS. IN THEIR TWO-YEAR LIFE SPAN, THEY ONLY EAT THREE BLOOD MEALS.

- Ticks have a sharp harpoon-like mouth so they can poke through skin to suck their meal. As the tick sucks, the belly expands like a giant balloon filling with blood.

- A tick may take several days to complete a blood meal. It then drops off the animal serving it dinner and digests.

- Ticks wait in tall grasses, bushes, or trees for a meal to stroll by. Carbon dioxide from breath or butyric acid from skin tell the tick that warm-blooded food is near.

- Lyme disease and Rocky Mountain spotted fever are diseases caused by ticks.

- Ticks sometimes hitch rides on migrating birds.

WORMS

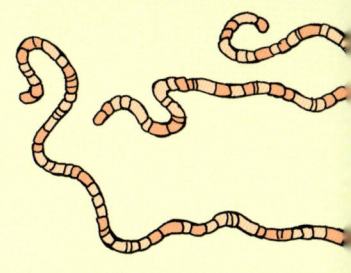

LOA LOA, OR THE AFRICAN EYE WORM, INFECTS HUMANS THROUGH FLY BITES. THE THIN ROUNDWORM CAN TRAVEL THOUGH THE BODY EATING TISSUE FLUID FOR YEARS. SOMETIMES IT CAN BE SEEN CRAWLING UNDER THE SKIN. ONLY IF THE WORM TRAVELS INTO THE EYE CAN IT BE REMOVED EASILY.

- The Guinea worm, or fiery serpent, enters humans if they drink contaminated water. The spaghetti-like worm can grow more than three feet long. When the worm wants to lay eggs, it pokes through the skin, usually of the leg or foot. The infected person feels terrible burning pain. The worm is removed bit by bit over many days.

- There are roundworms that live inside of dung beetles.

- Moth caterpillars can be infected with roundworms that release bacteria inside of their guts. The bacteria change the color of the caterpillar to red.

- A type of flatworm infects tadpoles in the area that will become legs. When the tadpole becomes a frog, it will have extra misshapen legs.

SPIDERS

THERE ARE ABOUT 25 MILLION TONS OF SPIDERS LIVING ON EARTH. THERE ARE AT LEAST 47,000 DIFFERENT TYPES OF SPIDERS, OR ARACHNIDS.

- A fear of spiders is called arachnophobia.

- The giant huntsman spider can have leg spans of almost one foot. The male giant huntsman spider sings a buzzy song to attract a female. Sometimes that attraction is fatal, as the female may eat the male after mating.

- Spiders eat insect-gut milkshakes. When spiders catch their dinner, they paralyze their prey with fangs, inject chemicals to dissolve the guts, then suck the guts out.

- The Goliath birdeater dines on large insects, worms, amphibians, and even birds.

- It can actually rain spiders. Spider rain, or mass ballooning, is when thousands of spiders float through the air on tiny strands of webbing. Spider rain fell in the Bay Area of California in 2023.

CRUNCHY AND CRUDDY
FLEAS

THERE ARE 2,500 DIFFERENT TYPES OF FLEAS. EACH KIND PREFERS A DIFFERENT BLOOD MEAL. IF YOU WERE A FLEA, WHICH KIND WOULD YOU BE? A HEN FLEA, DUCK FLEA, PIG FLEA, BADGER FLEA, BEAVER FLEA, RABBIT FLEA, SPARROW FLEA, DOG FLEA, CAT FLEA, MOUSE FLEA, OR A RAT FLEA?

- Fleas can jump 30,000 times without stopping.

- Jurassic fleas may have fed upon dinosaurs. These ancient fleas were big, ranging from 1/4 to 3/4 of an inch. Their mouthparts were armored with sawlike projections for getting blood from tough hides.

- Chigoes, or jiggers, are parasitic fleas that live in the sand of tropical areas. A pregnant female flea will burrow into a human foot. She feeds on blood and becomes full of eggs, which can cause her to grow up to 2,000 times her size. A very painful and itchy sore forms, which must be cut out.

- The cat flea can leap up eight inches. That is 150 times their body length. That would be the same as a four-foot person jumping from the ground to the roof of the Space Needle in Seattle, Washington.

- A flea can lift or drag stuff more than a hundred times its weight!

21

TERMITES

TERMITES FART! MICRO CREATURES LIVING IN THE GUT OF TERMITES HELP THEM DIGEST WOOD. THE MICRO CREATURES PRODUCE METHANE GAS, THE SAME GAS THAT HUMANS FART. THE TERMITES RELEASE THE GAS INTO THE AIR. TOOT!

- The worker termites from French Guiana in northeastern South America carry explosives on their backs. Glands grow sacks of blue crystals throughout their lives. If bitten, the crystal reacts with the enemy's spit. Boom! Dead enemy. Dead termite, too.

- Every terminate colony has only one queen. Her job is to lay eggs. She gets so full of eggs she cannot move and must be waited upon. In a single day, a queen termite can lay 30,000 eggs!

- The tallest termite mound ever recorded was found in the Republic of Congo in Africa. It was forty-two feet tall, as tall as a three-story building.

- One termite colony can have several million members. Scientists estimate that there are 10 quadrillion terminates worldwide. A quadrillion is 1 with fifteen zeros: 1,000,000,000,000,000.

23

24

BEETLES

THE BLISTER BEETLE IS A TYPE OF BEETLE THAT USED TO BE DRIED AND POWDERED AND THEN USED TO RAISE BLISTERS ON A PATIENT. THE PURPOSE WAS TO TREAT SKIN CONDITIONS LIKE WARTS.

- One out of every four animal species known on Earth is a beetle. There are more known species of beetles than species in the entire plant kingdom.

- The bombardier beetle squirts a hot, noxious spray of toxic bodily fluids, right out of its anus.

- To create these toxic fluids, the bombardier stores two chemicals separately in its abdomen. When the beetle squeezes a gland in its abdomen, the chemicals mix, react, and spew out of its butthole at an attacker.

- Tiger beetles from Australia can run eight feet a second. That would be the same as a racehorse running 500 miles an hour.

- The leaf beetle in Namibia feeds on the leaves of a very toxic plant. The San people in the Kalahari Desert squeeze toxin from the leaf beetle larvae onto arrow tips. The tiny tip of toxin can fell an antelope.

COCKROACHES

COCKROACHES THINK HUMANS ARE SO DISGUSTING THAT THEY WILL LICK THEMSELVES CLEAN AFTER A HUMAN TOUCH.

- German cockroaches ooze a chemical to draw in more cockroaches to make a crowd.

- A couple of Asian cockroaches can result in ten million roaches after one year. That is more cockroaches than people living in New York City.

- Cockroach droppings and dribbles make a room smell musty.

- Cockroaches pretty much eat anything, but they really like cinnamon rolls, white bread, and boiled potatoes.

- Cockroach blood is white.

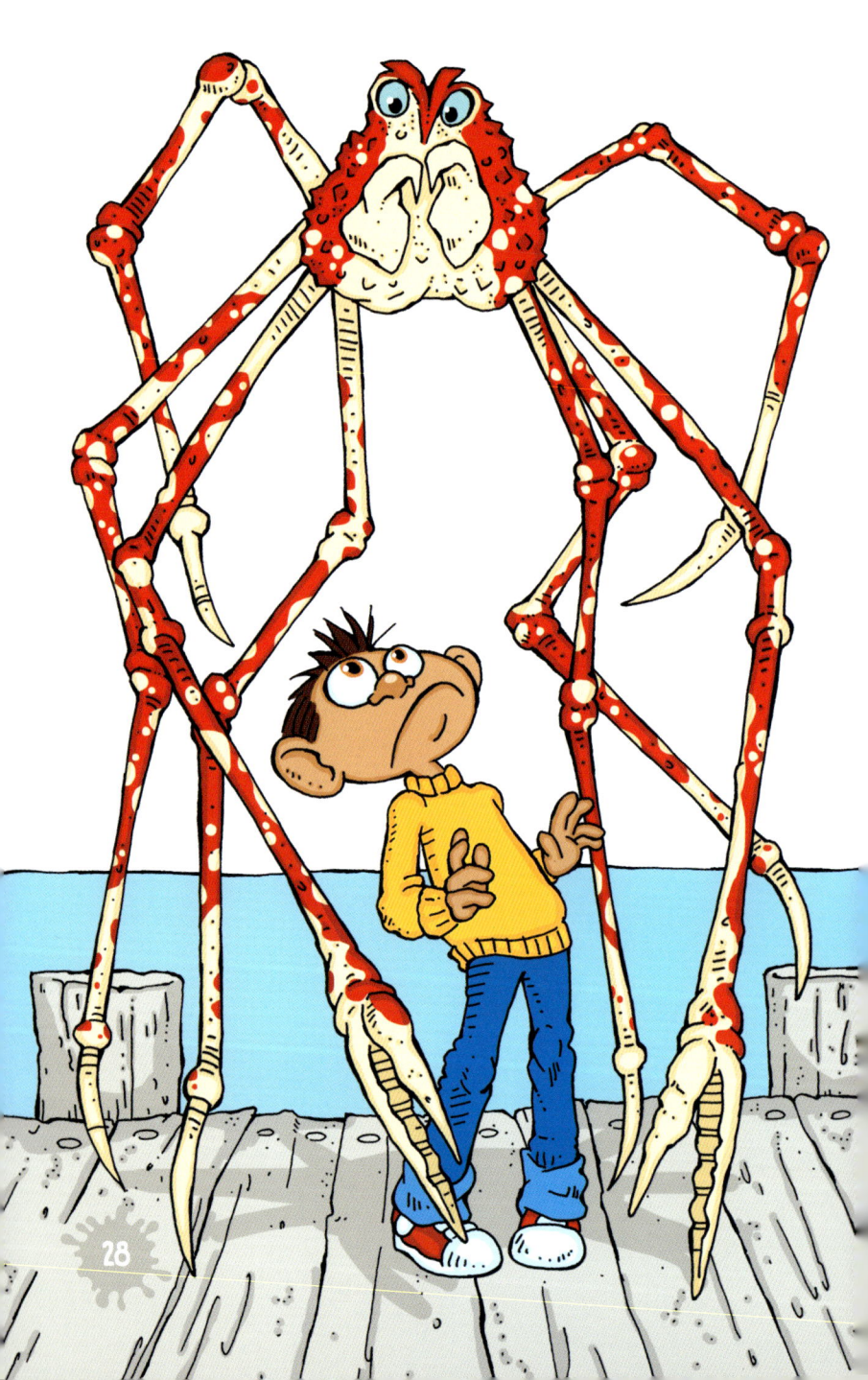

CRABS

HORSESHOE CRABS ARE BLUE-BLOODED. THEY HAVE COPPER IN THEIR BLOOD THAT GIVES IT A STYLISH BLUE COLOR WHEN EXPOSED TO AIR.

- The Japanese spider crab is huge! A large one can get up to twelve feet across from toe to toe and weigh up to forty-four pounds.

- The pea crab is very tiny. It is less than an inch long. Pea crabs live inside other sea creatures like oysters. Sometimes they live inside the butt of the sea cucumbers.

- Crabs grow by shedding their hard outer shells. So, the crab is squishy and soft until the new shell hardens. This can take hours or even days.

- Female crabs can release up to two thousand eggs at one time.

ANTS

ANTS CAN LIVE FOR A WEEK WITHOUT THEIR HEADS.

- The queen of an ant colony is the only one to have babies. When the eggs hatch into little wormlike larvae, she feeds them with liquid fat that she squirts out of her mouth.

- If an intruder insect enters an ant colony, the worker ants may hold the legs of the enemy while the soldier ants cut it in half.

- Army ants have large heads, long legs, strong jaws, and a painful sting. They do not nest. They move from place to place in swarms or long columns, devouring small prey like insects, lizards, frogs, and scorpions along the way. No, they don't eat humans!

- A type of tiny mite plugs itself into the end of an army ant's leg. It sucks blood as the ant uses the mite like a perfectly good foot.

- Fire ants can bite and sting at the same time and they attack en masse (meaning, as a huge group). They inject a venom that feels like burning.

SLIMY AND STICKY
FROGS

THE HAIRY FROG, OR HORROR FROG, BREAKS ITS OWN TOE BONES WHEN THREATENED. THE BONES PUNCTURE THROUGH THE SKIN TO MAKE A SET OF CATLIKE CLAWS.

- After mating, the male Darwin frog gathers up the eggs and stores them in his vocal sac. After the eggs develop into tiny frogs, the daddy frog belches them out into the world.

- The female Australian brooding frog swallows her fertilized eggs. She doesn't eat for the five weeks that her froglets develop.

- The common green frog can gobble up to 10,000 flies in a single summer.

- Glass frogs from Central and South America are lime green on top, but they are see-through on the underside. You can see the organs inside their bodies.

33

TOADS

TOADS MAY LOOK ALL BUMPY AND WARTY, BUT NOPE, YOU CAN'T GET WARTS FROM TOUCHING A TOAD.

- The largest toad ever found was in an Australian national park. The cane toad weighed almost six pounds and was twenty-one inches long. The park rangers nicknamed her Toadzilla.

- Toads have poison glands on their skin that can sicken animals that try to eat them. Their poison can make humans sick, too. Poison from the cane and Colorado River toads can make people nauseated and dizzy, and even cause heart attacks. So, touching toads won't give you warts, but it could make you very sick.

- Surinam toads are very flat with bumpy backs. This female toad carries her fertilized eggs embedded in little pockets under the skin on her back. When the toadlets are born, they burst through their mother's skin, kind of like popping pimples.

FISH

CANDIRU FISH ARE ABOUT AN INCH LONG AND TOOTHPICK THIN. THEY SWIM UP THE GILLS OF FISH IN THE AMAZON RIVER TO FEED ON FISH BLOOD.

- Herring fish fart at night by squeezing gas bubbles out of their anal pores. The researchers said it sounds like someone blowing raspberries.

- Puffer fish inflate themselves into balls by swallowing large amounts of water or air to stop attackers. Most of them are also extremely poisonous. However, this doesn't stop adventurous diners in Japan from eating fugu, or puffer fish.

- Yummy, yummy fish eggs! Caviar is salted fish eggs. Caviar can be very expensive. Two ounces, or enough for two tablespoons, can cost hundreds of dollars.

- Lamprey are long eel-shaped fish. Their razor-sharp teeth gnaw through skin. Their sucking mouths attach so they can slurp up a blood meal. Even swimmers have been attacked!

38

SNAILS

THE OFFICIAL NAME FOR SNAIL SLIME IS MUCUS.

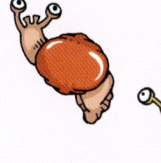

- Snail slime allows a snail to go over rocks, sticks, even broken glass without harm. It also allows the snail to travel up, down, and even upside down.

- In 2002, a large group of snails invaded a neighborhood in Brazil and covered houses in slime!

- Snails have both male and female parts. So, when two snails mate, they both make eggs.

- People eat snails, but they call it escargot. May 24 is National Escargot Day.

- Snails withdraw into their shells and seal the opening to sleep through long dry periods. Some Mexican desert snails slept for six years in the drawer of a scientist.

SEA CUCUMBERS

SEA CUCUMBERS ARE SHAPED LIKE THEIR NAMESAKE, WITH WARTY, SLIMY, POISONOUS SKIN.

- Sea cucumbers breathe through their butthole and use it to deposit waste as well. Sometimes pearlfish live inside their butthole.

- One type of sea cucumber develops its young in the anus.

- If threatened, some sea cucumbers will shoot long, gooey strings from the butthole. The attacker becomes wound up in the goo threads.

- A really scared sea cucumber may blow its guts out of its butthole. The sea cucumber then crawls away and grows new insides.

- A thick, gelatinous soup is made from sea cucumbers. Sometimes sea cucumber intestines in seawater are sipped as a health drink.

42

BIRD DOO-DOO

BIRD DROPPINGS CONTAIN BOTH POO AND PEE. THEY ARE FULL OF A CHEMICAL CALLED URIC ACID AND OTHER SALTS BUT VERY LITTLE WATER. THE CHEMICALS IN BIRD DOO CAN BE SO STRONG THAT IT CAN DESTROY CAR PAINT.

- Herons, gulls, and storks bring bits of food long distances to feed their young. Because it can be difficult to carry, the parent birds eat the food then puke it up later into the mouths of their babies.

- Hawk, owl, and raven babies stick their rear ends over the edge of their nests to squirt out dookie.

- Owls eat their food whole. They cannot digest fur, bones, feathers, or scales. The undigested bits form into a pellet and the bird barfs them out. An owl pellet often contains the complete skeletons of the animals the owl had for dinner.

- In the 1970s, peregrine falcons were reintroduced to the eastern United States. Researchers noticed the birds liked cliff nesting sites with thick white stains from bird poop. So, the researchers splotched cliffs with fake bird whitewash (white paint) to attract the falcons.

SALAMANDERS

SALAMANDERS LOOK LIKE SLIMY LIZARDS. THEY ARE COVERED IN MUCUS THAT IS POISONOUS IF SWALLOWED.

- If salamanders lose a limb, they can grow a new one.

- Salamanders are cannibals. They will gladly eat other salamanders that are smaller than themselves.

- Chinese giant salamanders can grow up to almost six feet long and weigh up to 110 pounds.

- The Chinese giant salamander oozes a white goo if threatened or injured. Researchers used this mucus to make glue for sticking skin together after surgeries.

- The fire salamander does not lay eggs but gives live birth to tiny little salamanders.

- The Texas blind salamander has no eyes, only two black dots under the skin.

SMELLY AND SCARY
SPRAY

MILLIPEDES, STINK BUGS, LADYBUGS, AND BEDBUGS ALL RELEASE A SMELLY SPRAY WHEN DISTURBED.

- Tapirs can spray urine backward seven to ten feet when they pee.

- Hippos use their tail as twirling propellors to spray poop around. They do this to mark their territory.

- Skunks are the champions of the stinky spray. Skunk spray is so strong, it can make humans vomit. The only animals that usually prey on skunks are those with a weak sense of smell, like great horned owls.

- An octopus under attack sprays ink into the water. The ink confuses the attacker and allows the octopus to escape. The ink may also affect the predator's sense of smell and taste.

DOOKIE

MOTHER GORILLAS EAT THE POO OF THEIR BABIES FOR THE FIRST FOUR TO SIX MONTHS OF THE INFANT GORILLA'S LIFE.

- Dung beetles have been feeding on animal poo for a very long time. When a paleontologist was cutting into a large fossilized hadrosaur poop, she found burrows made by dung beetles.

- You can purchase field guides for identifying wild animal caca, or scat. This way you too can experience the joys of scatology—the study of animal droppings.

- Wildlife researcher Olaus Murie gathered a scat collection that contained more than 1,200 specimens.

- Doo-doo from wild dogs and cats look a lot like the poop from Rover and Kitty, except they may contain hair, bones, and fur.

- Rabbit pellets are round. Deer pellets are more pointed.

49

SCENTS

MANY ANIMALS USE URINE TO MARK TERRITORY. CATS, DOGS, WOLVES, FOXES, BEAVERS, MICE, AND HYENAS ALL LEAVE PEE SIGNS TO SAY, "STAY OFF OF MY TURF!"

- The musk deer uses scent to attract females. People like the smell, too. Musk cologne is based on the same scent as the male musk deer. Probably not a good idea to wear that cologne when hiking in musk deer country.

- One type of cockroach leaves behind a scent that smells like maraschino cherries.

- Ants leave behind a trail of scent for other fellow ants to follow.

- Like skunks, weasels and wolverines spew a stink for defense. Phew!

52

FARTS

THE SONORAN CORAL SNAKE AND THE WESTERN HOOK-NOSED SNAKE FART! IF FRIGHTENED, THEY BOTH FART BY PUSHING AIR THROUGH THEIR CLOACAL SPHINCTER, OR SNAKE WASTE HOLE. THE FARTS SOUND LIKE HUMAN FARTS BUT A BIT HIGHER IN PITCH.

- The western hook-nosed snake can fart so hard that it flings itself off of the ground.

- Sea lions have really stinky farts that smell like rotten fish. No surprise, since that is what they eat.

- Birds do not need to fart.

- You cannot hear rat farts but you can smell them. The smell depends upon what they have been eating, just as with humans.

- Whales fart—and their farts are very big.

- Zebras fart constantly. It is because of how their body digests food. When running away from a predator, they poot with every stride.

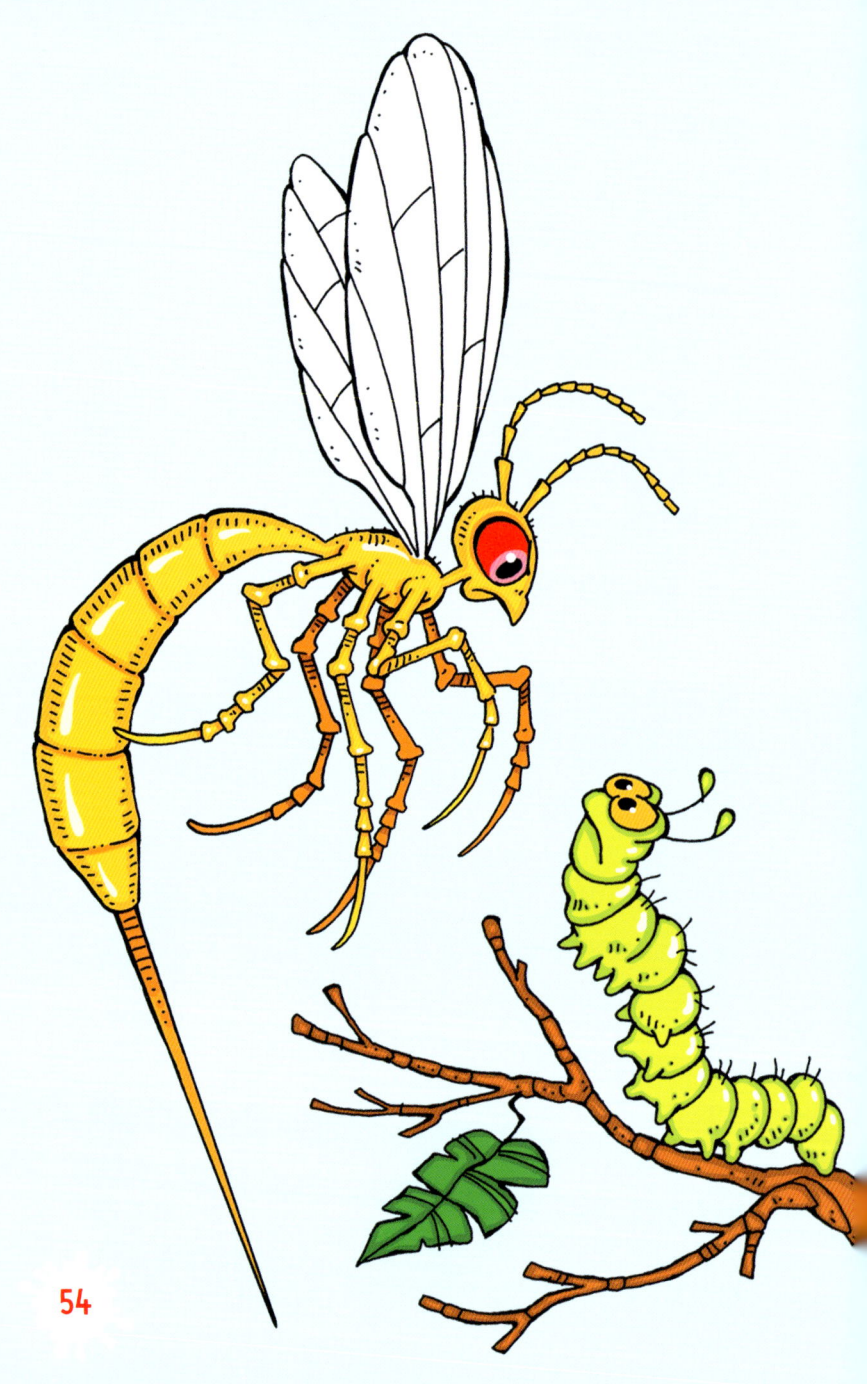

PARASITES

THE TONGUE-EATING LOUSE FINDS A HOME INSIDE OF A FISH MOUTH. IT FEEDS ON THE BLOOD OF THE FISH TONGUE UNTIL IT WITHERS AWAY. THE LOUSE THEN ATTACHES TO THE TONGUE STUB. THE FISH NOW HAS A LOUSE FOR A TONGUE AND THE LOUSE HAS A FISH TO SUCK BLOOD FROM.

- A minute species of sea snail starts out tiny, but once one finds the butthole of a sea cucumber, it sheds its organs except for the wormlike egg-laying part. This odd snail acts like a tapeworm, absorbing nutrients and spewing eggs from the sea cucumber's anus.

- March 4 is Parasite Day.

- Parasitoid wasps lay eggs inside caterpillars, fly pupae, and adult insects. They slowly kill the host as they develop by eating away the insides. When grown, they chew their way out.

- The movie *Alien* was supposedly inspired by parasitoid wasps.

- There is a type of parasitoid wasp that preys upon the larvae of other parasitoid wasps.

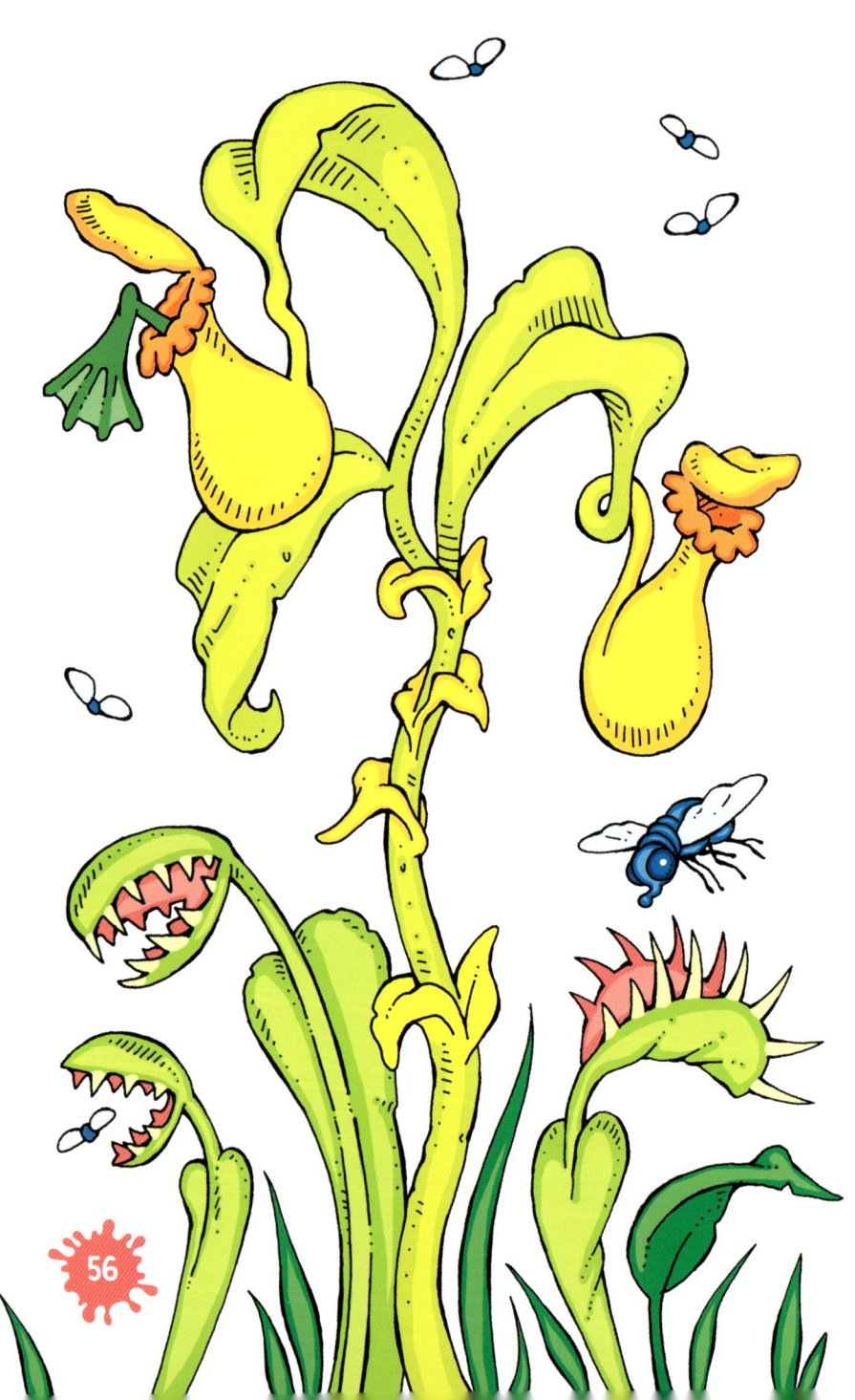

FLESH-EATING PLANTS

PITCHER PLANTS CAN EAT FROGS! EXCEPT THEY CAN'T DIGEST THE SKIN ON THE FEET. SO LITTLE FROGGIE SLIPPERS ARE LEFT INSIDE.

- The Venus flytrap looks like it has a little mouth. If a bug flies in, the mouth closes.

- The cobra lily has clear spots in their leaves. The bug thinks it is escaping but instead, it is going deeper into the plant.

- The Australian sundew looks like it has little drops of water on the end of stalks. But the drops are not water; they are a sticky glue that traps their insect meal.

- The largest of the pitcher plants can trap and eat rodents.

- The bat pitcher plant lives on bat dookie, or guano. It has a ridge that bats roost upon. The plant kind of acts as a bat toilet bowl.

- There are more than seven hundred different kinds of meat-eating plants in the world.

57

BATS

THERE ARE 1,400 DIFFERENT SPECIES OF BAT WORLDWIDE.

- Bats use their wings to scoop up insects.

- In one night, bats can eat their body weight in insects. That would be like a person eating twenty pizzas in one night.

- A bite or a scratch from a bat can give a person rabies.

- Most bats eat insects. But some also eat fish, frogs, mice, and birds. Then there are nectar-drinking bats. And of course, the blood-slurping vampire bats.

- Bat poo is harvested and used as a fertilizer. In the 1800s, bat guano was mined from caves to make gunpowder.

RATS

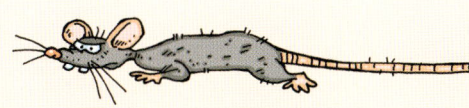

A GROUP OF RATS IS CALLED A MISCHIEF.

- A single rat can leave 25,000 droppings a year. That is a whole lot of poo.

- There are seventy different rat species. It is estimated that there is one rat for every human in the world.

- Rats pretty much eat anything. If the food supply runs out, they will eat one another.

- There are more than twenty-five diseases that rats can spread to humans.

- Sumatran bamboo rats are the largest rats in the world. Their bodies can reach twenty inches and they can weigh almost nine pounds, or about the size of an infant baby boy.

SNAKES

ALTHOUGH NOT A VERY COMMON OCCURRENCE, A STRESSED SNAKE MAY BITE ITS OWN TAIL AND START EATING ITSELF.

- Snake jaws open wide so they can swallow their prey whole. And really big snakes, like pythons, can eat really big animals. Pythons have been known to eat alligators, deer, and even people.

- Ilha da Queimada Grande, or Snake Island, off the coast of Brazil is home for two to four thousand golden lancehead vipers, one of the deadliest snakes in the world. Their venom can melt human flesh. No one lives there and tourists are not allowed on the island.

- The most toxic snake in the world is the inland taipan from Australia. The venom from one bite could be enough to kill one hundred humans.

- A snake head can still bite after it has been chopped off.

- Snakes can fly! Or, rather, glide. So-called flying snakes actually jump from trees. When in the air they flatten their bodies and make wavelike motions like they are swimming. A flying snake can land seventy feet away from the launch site.